DIRGE

A Ballet For 13 Dancers

Krysia Jopek

"Earth as detritus, beckons language of its turmoil . . . . ***DIRGE*** is a swept windstorm among the assemblages of our times, an unfurling rhizome for survival."

Edwin Torres

"In the dance, what is implicate unfolds only to surrender once more to the whole. ***DIRGE*** moves, lives at the difficult, intimate cusp of knowing, which is also the cusp of being. Embodied, [illegible]illed, [un]veiled, spent, its insights evanesce and yet, like all [illegible]n[illegible]ity, linger."

Sharon Lattig

"Is metaphysical hopscotch a stage for modern ballet?
condensed, relational, generative as fructifying?
so full of life and kindness are these ballets,
it's easy to forget they're dirges…"

Chris Stroffolino

First Edition, May 2024
Library of Congress Control Number: 2024933941
ISBN 978-1-953136-05-3 Hardback
ISBN 978-1-953136-53-4 Paperback

Cover Design by Kurt Lovelace
Cover Art by Pierian Springs Press
Cover type ***Bauhaus Dessau*** **Alfarn** by Céline Hurka,
Elia Preuss, Flavia Zimbardi,
Hidetaka Yamasaki, and Luca Pellegrini.
Poetry title and body set in ***URW*** **Baskerville.**
Misc. in **Jenson** by Robert Slimbach & **Sabon** by Jan Tschichold.
Flourishes set in Emigre Foundry **Dalliance**, by Frank Heine &
Emigre Foundry **ZeitGuys**, by Bob Aufuldish, Eric Donelan.
Typefaces licensed Adobe, Linotype, & URW GmbH.

PSPress.Pub
Pierian Springs Press, Inc
30 N Gould St, Ste 30
Sheridan, Wyoming 82801

"Sculptured memories and reflections tantalize in a spectral ballet like wisps of smoke; the analytical reflection inside such undercurrents is delicious work for the reader. Complexity and diversity of conscious life can be imagined as generously flashing before the eyes—as in a last, desperately drawn out, critical moment."

Miguel Escobar

"Jopek's words will have you gripped in a sensation to host your own shadow in the beauty of your own brokenness."

Sheikha A

"Language is the house of the truth of being."

Martin Heidegger
Poetry, Language, Thought

"I am now fallen; stardust envelops me."

Virginia Woolf
The Waves

For you who hold this book

"Everything that is dead quivers. Not only the things of poetry, stars, moon, wood, flowers, but even a white trouser."

Wassily Kandinsky
Concerning the Spiritual in Art

"A painting is not about an experience. It is an experience. Art is an adventure into an unknown world, which can be explored only by those willing to take risks. Art to me is an anecdote of the spirit, and the only means of making concrete the purpose of its varied quickness and stillness."

Mark Rothko
Writings on Art

PROGRAM

DIRGE (n.)

\ ˈdərj \

1. a song or hymn of grief or lamentation, especially one intended to accompany funeral or memorial rites; a funeral DIRGE
2. a slow, solemn, and mournful piece of music
3. something (such as a poem) that has the qualities of a DIRGE

DIRGE

A Ballet For 13 Dancers

Dancers

August

Bunny

Canto

Fresno

Haiti

Hayden

Hazel

Moonbeam

Orpheus

Plato

Stearns

Temple

Wolf

Prelude
With Cellos

1 dancer:
Hazel

I slept in the Book of the Dead and woke with parchment scrolls
blooming tired magnolias from my unhinged mouth.

Lugubrious cellos attempted to climb me back to the mud-
encrusted, stone floor—but I panicked.

When my thinking can trace some semblance of surface,
I might explain.

Some will pigeonhole me verbose.

If I erase, the Dreams of the Dead multiply.

First Movement in G Minor

I

The Green Room

13 dancers:
August, Bunny, Canto, Fresno, Haiti, Hayden,
Hazel, Moonbeam,Orpheus, Plato, Stearns, Temple, Wolf

When the dreams were cremated on Saturday, they left white ash in our hair.

The ghosts hid the small deaths—watching us.

It was odd: the leave-taking, micro-swimming the rain, shaking fallen coats, making room for Room.

August couldn't abandon incongruity with any knock-on-the-front-door kind of wisdom.

We were one and another then, floating paintings—pretending we weren't too tired to want anything.

If the operation had been successful, the stranger's kidney would become family.

Disease, you know, can gnaw lungs.

The afterworld might be a softened spectacle.

A liquid palette that proliferates.

Imperatives might prove useful even if discarded much later with shattered birdhouses.

You should alert the neighbors about the accident.

Ignore the hyacinths that didn't bloom, the gardenias devoid of petal-scent—

the gardeners at the back of the stage sobbing in empty watering cans.

When you drink the sea, too tired to tread the surface,

the gods instruct: float with your torso, recite the alphabet in reverse, create a new classification system for your memories.

A composition can cause disarray.

The maestro's hands have been bartered for falcon wings.

Someone threw out the metronome.

G Minor is the saddest key, but there's no translation for your feelings.

Our most accomplished choreographers can expose the rubble of the poorest countries,

the collapse of currencies that can no longer purchase the sea's reflection.

Shhh!

You mustn't say anything about the Victorian Gothic, Sci-fi set.

The sculptor went a little crazy.

You should note the 4 emergency exits in the event of an active shooter.

Those in the cheaper seats may be asked for donations of blood.

Thirteen characters are busy exchanging personalities in the dressing room—

The writers are rearranging pages.

Note: all your seats recline.

The mosaic tiles on the floor contain mirrors.

Debilitated fisherwomen, teal sea glass in their throats, count days of impossible catch,

sponge salt from decaying lips—sing in fractured sixteenth notes,

palimpsest-ing hymns.

Please don't talk about—the narrative fray!—

until the final cymbal crash.

Canto, the catbird, perched in the high-pitched eaves, calculates your every move.

His marble eyes, those of a miniature goat or wolf, have locked the stranger's eyes in the front row—gray, by default.

Don't be alarmed.

Ensconced, the ambulances tread 911.

Call a priest who can't answer.

Wake the sleep-laden soothsayer.

Notify your person—though Wi-Fi reception might be shoddy, given the lightning and hail.

Three philosophers are playing with Playdoh in an absurd sandbox, but we're not naming names.

It's good for you to spend quality time in dirt.

Meaning?

Let's not get ahead of ourselves.

Syllogisms might concave.

The dancers should get ready in the green room for this

DIRGE—for the spinning firefly disco lights—

Go!

We're pitching sky.

The sun is spinning hieroglyphics.

It's time to climb up from your abyss with a brand-new wish list.

Throw rice at the submerged iPhone at the bottom of the stolen car ditched in the dirty river.

Roll down the windows for shallow air.

Prepare white funerary cloths in the event of a bleeding out after extrication.

Are you ready?

We're one series of equations away from a possible vacation—maybe a catharsis, let's say.

The Chorus is looking subtle but regal—drawing cards from a magical deck.

Note: it's imperative to jettison this Book based on good behavior.

You've been very patient—you, with your pockets inside out.

II

The Afterlife Smells Like Ghosts

7 dancers:
August, Hayden, Hazel, Orpheus, Plato, Stearns, Temple

Everyone slows down and locks the rearview mirror when the ambulance arrives.

Demise crosshatches the body's sleeves.

How funny I look without skin.

Lacking the memory of other cells, the cell is lonely.

Inconsolable, the violas slip off the page.

A gamelan can be ordered on Amazon.

Rumors perforate.

No one calls now that I've given up color.

It was an intense exercise in inflection before I straggled here.

Metaphors and allegory atrophied.

I lost my hypothesis, so I opened the divine with a can opener.

I didn't want to spoil.

I was exhausted from being a pronoun.

A new language can't be created overnight.

Burdens design their own burdening.

The one who overdosed stopped looking for God.

There were questionable assumptions.

Footnotes to Sunday might be muddled under bulldozers.

The fix contained Fentanyl.

The cornfield collected us in silk.

The ghosts say believe, but they don't say what.

Sleep doesn't even know.

The day job had the subject tunneling through rusted filing cabinets.

Outside old men were bartering dominos in those margins of wind people fall through at stop signs.

You should feed this duck, but not another—drink this water, wake that mother,

remind another without telling the other, that you're disproportionate—and afraid.

The doctors can sing your prognosis if that will help.

Your idiosyncrasies are replicating as we speak.

A bad habit can become a ritual without an underpinning.

You're stranger than before.

He said, you're a sheet of glass in a windy city.

He said, bring the small turtle because it knows how to hide.

If we see each other at the border, don't say anything.

War can't explain daylight.

It's your right not to watch.

It's more difficult to play dead than you think.

Tell the children they're statues but can't sculpt their own until the game is over—until they return to school.

That the soldiers won't wake up in the moonlight.

Tell tomorrow you're not as selfish as yesterday.

Protect the eighty-seven-foot papyrus scroll from any incendiary material.

Strangely, one arranges another.

Things here don't hurt so much.

Grief is a different color, and sadness doesn't own a house.

I raised my hand to ask profound questions, but everyone left for happy hour—somewhere less confusing.

Was it too much?

—all my information, contemplation, eradication, promulgation, spiritual espionage?

I've forgotten how to spell.

No one will find me with autocorrect.

The field of dandelions is clover—the lover, over.

A neurosurgeon extracts desire that has become unbecoming.

You should try harder to stay still.

Events take place in seams.

The afterlife smells like ghosts, an echo in syntax's coiled pinfold.

It's not a pinwheel or windmill, he said.

The ghosts sob in attic cobwebs, converse with slippery bats.

They advise, go slow across the broken stone tablets—climb over your missing feet.

Here you don't need your stolen teeth, emerald scarabs, a lucky rabbit's foot—all that trigonometry.

There were kinetic misunderstandings—a fallout of composure.

You should have checked the batteries in the fire alarm.

What did you expect for a dollar?

That the compass you gave your son would still glow chartreuse in the dark.

That he would find his way out without you.

Someone more credentialed will execute the laborious paper chain from a cork-board cubicle.

I'm over here! —peering over the half-wall.

We've gone ahead with your last wishes despite how macabre—

or was that a typo?

If you're holding onto a couple of Aces and a King, you won't feel a thing.

Someone with war medals and the utmost stoicism will be qualified to bury most of your despair.

There's ice cream for everyone, said the Emperor.

Pancakes might cheer you up.

Before you give everything away: your warmest down coat, your food provisions, bread for the birds, your idealism—

you should save something for yourself.

There might be semantic delay.

Plato, what did Socrates say?

Hemlock was his choice.

The chalice was laced with envy.

Someone stepped on his spectacles.

Sanity became opaque.

Only some of this matters.

This time we're going somewhere on high-speed train cars with no passengers.

The panoramic scenery, city to city, is breathtaking—

volumes of photos no one prints or saves.

At the next stop someone might say something like:

Bedouins read stones, pitched stairs escalate, or mannequins split our dreams.

Leading a camel to water doesn't make anyone noble.

Even if we sing in languages we don't understand.

At the next stop, I might feel like going home.

At the next city, I might sign declarations with invisible ink.

I might mean everything I don't remember.

III

Empty Temples

12 dancers:
August, Bunny, Canto, Haiti, Hayden, Hazel, Moonbeam, Orpheus, Plato, Stearns, Temple, Wolf

Night pulled new hostages down for the dream world, a dozen at a time.

Stones are heavy before they become blackbirds.

Some gods are too hungry to pluck another's hunger.

Their black eyes, collecting painful souvenirs.

Ideas became objects that overfilled the House.

The House mocked the ideas the objects lost.

Desire's sequence of footsteps cluttered Monday's cartography.

Someone's OCD kicked in at 3:17 AM.

You were neurotically restaging events in your living room, unable to peel layers down.

Shadow boxes, random words in exotic calligraphy, strange phrases, obsolete instruments of travel,

photos of ancient ruins, empty temples, doors that didn't go anywhere.

In the desert the mirage was a sign of confusion, normalized by the gathering sandstorm.

A bevy of lutes, wooden flutes, and techno-violins braided a red-noon estuary.

I babysat your sadness last night and left before you woke—

handing off the baton to the restless ghosts of your house that find you charming.

When I fell prostrate at the temple floor, I lost myself in empty spaces.

Until I pulled my entire city of birds down.

To show you how the poem celebrates its staccato-chords—

realizing too late that this had become too cerebral.

In the Book you're writing—someone continues sending
unfinished stories that follow like a dream
that keeps beginning—

even though you keep waking.

In the Diaries of the Somnambulist every dream is a new City, a magic Room in a House that extrapolates us—

City of Imperfect Circles, City of Y, City Where I Invented You.

In a Lost City, gamelans play a DIRGE for the princess who stopped eating, disappeared.

Chance deals a joker under Plato's ideal table that isn't the King's jester.

You should make sure she doesn't carry weapons.

The borders, as usual, are questionable.

Everyone was trying to get out of town, see themselves from somewhere else, less unsettling.

It's okay to be lost on one-way streets, working in the dark, one of us said—

filling out paperwork with your name, so you can belong.

Once we cauterize the bleeding, you'll be wiser.

Once on the highest floor of the skyscraper, your image shall multiply.

You now live on Choice Street in the City of Renewal in a state called Mild Chaos, and work for the Department of Speculation.

I know you're wondering about all this—

once you come to terms with terms you created haphazardly.

Inhabitants of an ancient city gather at the elastic perimeter to hold the world in place.

They take turns on a deadly pilgrimage to the center—to trampoline back to gods and goddesses, they think.

The ones who don't return by curfew are burned in the sun.

Performance can take wrong turns.

After I became an envelope for myself, the subject said—

I cut out my heart with a kitchen knife because it no longer served me,

sheathed it in the music box the wind broke with the miniature ballerina splayed.

I set the clock back against the salt pond's shimmering mirrors

to another twilight when someone held me against starlight.

Nothing is forever except forever.

It's the proper time to sit the ghosts down and tell them
everything.

They're afraid for you.

I didn't mean to run the car in the garage.

It became difficult to find things worth finding.

I didn't mean to pretend to be incredulous, dubious, misguided,
dangerous, make the locals stare—

shift solace away from itself.

One of us proffered a Book on a silver tray
of watery moonlight—

a Book inside a Book inside a House inside a House

of being—quiet, quelled.

No longer a quotient.

We should confess to imperfection's diligence, chart ingrained woes in chalk against obscurity.

Murals in Brazil's favelas rush downhill in the rainy season, leave visual echoes.

I found the missing encryption to unlock the afternoon, but then I misplaced it again.

Now we're between chapters, the divisions on vinyl between songs.

Now the sky tells a story of sky—until we forget what the sky has told us.

The characters in the ensemble have jumped off the stage, abandoning store-bought salvation.

A line of questionable propriety is always personal.

I don't feel like capitalism anymore, one of us said.

No one else will understand—all the gaps between
y and z, the ending—

a circular mouth on syllables resurrecting sound.

The ghosts drown out our words—jealous we can speak them.

Electric cellos in empty temples turn Bach
into a madman for an hour or two.

The Chorus choreographs us:

dismantle the clocks—and breathe.

At the altar—on landmines.

The body never sleeps in the same Room.

Verbs in the story fall out.

Being = an event.

The film on consciousness defines it.

The text I'm writing [disappears].

IV

Metaphysical Hopscotch

4 dancers:
Bunny, Hayden, Hazel, Plato

We played metaphysical hopscotch on Hemlock Street.

I couldn't get past 5 without ending in sink holes.

My favorite paperweight disappeared overnight
with one velvet slipper.

The dog slept on 7 because he was bored.

My body outgrew itself like an onion, a floating target of crested bluebirds flying home.

Orpheus played the guitar to appease dissonance.

One chord became a mystic.

I slept in a diaphanous cocoon
because my deceased father told me.

The spine of the Book mutated into a snow butterfly.

When the pages evaporated, I became air.

In an unknown city, identity is stolen by cracked sidewalks.

The wallet traded for a computerized watch.

The passwords purposely disremembered.

My name is Joy, Storm, Willow, Stone.

There's a scattering of dusk's muted stained glass in the forest.

No one can explain.

Gunshots in the distance, hardly noticeable at all, but
perimeters are porous.

Strangers will commiserate as if they'll be friends but will never
see each other again.

The Book of Sorrows placed on the shelf abutting the ceiling
that requires a missing ladder.

The Dictionary of Longing secured under the bed where the cat
hides when it rains.

If I flail philosophically, the outer sky might gather the slack, impel algorithms, fractal stars.

All lines cast wouldn't offer a silver shad—one amber eye finding us.

No one meant to leave you so stripped down, nihilistic.

I made up my mind, but it turned itself back, mythologically.

No emotional atlas existed on the coffee table.

When you solve the enigma, it ceases to exist.

We were jealous of another's travel—circumventing volcanoes for theology.

A few beheld time illusory in golden hammocks.

You were worried about us, and we laughed in the wrong direction—

traveling in reverse on a circuitous train, inventing new names for objects we wouldn't remember.

Not everything aches at once, but cascades.

Hired to play sonatas to tire the insomniac, the pianist falls asleep on the high keys and dreams of daffodils.

The insomniac smokes a cigar in a room of books he'll never read but finds comforting—all those veiled sentences.

Ambiguity makes some members of the audience uncomfortable.

I didn't want a ticket to this.

How abstract some aspects had become.

We could love each other, but we're too poor to own words.

The last time we spoke, I told a few lies I don't remember.

Something, maybe ontology, had to be sacrificed.

Everything was disconcerting at times, but time didn't follow every path lost on the mountain.

We smoothed out the logic in arrears for those nervous the time would be up, nowhere to go.

Removed from the garbage, the broken cello becomes a hollow drum in the north end—where sirens punctuate sketchy poker games.

The foreign coins in our pockets from a country where we may have loved are useless—now that we fear conclusions.

Programmed to explicate literary texts, the robot crumbles as if crying before the necessary reboot.

Damn it.

We were so close.

Maybe it was the unavailable context, the sailboat unmoored by the unexpected typhoon.

They should have studied the squirrels.

They should have worn the neon lifejackets.

There was no avalanche of hurry now that our bodies were transposing wings.

We rose anointed until the oil on our foreheads evaporated.

I can't sleep because I might fall back into the Book of the Dead,

become a plaintive ballet inverted.

The next time we speak, I won't tell you about the frozen rabbit
in the garden—

its legs perched in Arctic air after rigor mortis set in.

Or how I burned twenty-six letters, your favorite scarf.

I might tell you I miss the person you wanted to become before
you slipped into trees.

Now that you know all this, maybe you'll come back to tell
stories of the future without any disclaimer, emotional cost.

I'll confess how I'm learning to abbreviate myself.

I'm twirling tulips.

I'm bathing the woman who sings.

I'm skiing internal ice.

I'm a sailboat in the forest.

I'm counting perfect angles.

I'm diagonal.

I knew something.

I digress.

V

Feathers of Yellow Wings Desire Thumbprints

5 dancers:
Bunny, Hazel, Plato, Stearns, Wolf

Distance arrows memory with aperture.

We're relearning to be yellow, an impulse stitching phosphorous.

The last black-eyed Susans wilt the garden because we've neglected to climb outside.

A Mobïus strip absconds with materialism.

Clowns weep into festive plastic cups, plan their retirements on the Galapagos Islands.

Lost in residual forests, the excommunicated soothsayer feeds goldfinches from ripped bell-sleeves.

No magical hat returns the zeret bird to orchards of silver olive trees.

I'm sorry for what we have done tomorrow.

The yellow feathers may succumb to the dog's mouth.

Wedding money might go missing.

There will be a suicide somewhere.

Don't ask too many questions.

Song that is wanted is still song, said the deaf woman.

A missing hand wants a shadow.

Perched in the pines, the owl continues writing its sestina.

Buddha's terracotta chin and left ear are injured indefinitely
because none of us can locate industrial glue.

I've put yellow duct tape around our former happiness.

I wrote you, but that was three email addresses ago.

I was cognitively flatlining.

What happened?

Everything and nothing.

The soundtrack crashed.

I slept under September without dreaming.

The kitchen calendar of exotic waterfalls was hidden.

Furniture fell through my head: a lacquered dining room table, a granite desk, a ceiling fan.

Someone said, you have alibis.

Bunny says, people miss you.

The House says, there's daylight here.

The birds say, we're waiting.

The morning says, you should come back.

The wind says, no one should wander alone so much.

Get a second opinion.

Thin tree branches still feather towards the summer sun.

I could turn this all around, but I can't.

I'm too parallel.

Let's recycle what we said, the other said—before your eyes became marigolds.

Someone should pull the thin seeds and save them in a sealed envelope labeled: maybe next year.

Someone should say something that is not trite.

The elephant in the room was unlucky.

The hunter isn't contrite on social media.

Not all entertainment can be determined inside someone's head, a game of make believe, a spilling over.

Call a tenured logician to weigh in from a sleeping villa on the Mediterranean.

Wires in the brain couldn't be untangled until it was too late to determine how sorry the subject was.

Bystanders were interviewed for novel comments, claims.

Some members of the Chorus were taking notes for Twitter.

Weeping willows despise gravity.

The ghosts dream of walking barefoot, balanced on sun-warmed temple stones.

They don't take all their memories with them.

The memory of death is written without hands.

More determinations of inclines, protractors, will be set against shrinking skies—

while Monarch butterflies slip through the wrong nets.

The children's babysitters are sorry, unfurling dragon kites.

Out of necessity, passages of hours may become throw-away.

Not every day wants to be a poem.

We hung our best selves on poor-quality video, eluding face-recognition software.

For stealing her name, the subject attempts to suffocate her doppelgänger with a gluttony that terrifies them both.

Some of us find a niche, but there's no one to confide in.

Gilgamesh sleeps through immortality.

Narcissus drowns because the beloved gazed back at him with an intensity he couldn't bear.

If the debacle had been planned properly, we could still do lunch.

There should be a word for someone who blows up consecutive bridges with one damp match.

Someone like you.

Fire can be gratifying like empiricism.

Some discursions became fluid—what was thought, spiraling into an extraordinary, let's say, event.

Even now, you meander quite eloquently.

When you're looking in the wrong places, it's time
to stop looking.

White lying can alleviate boredom, preempt
hassles of description.

This time, it's best for all parties to become fluent in silence.

No one else needs to review your psychological scorecard.

Icarus never wept.

His waxen wings singe the conductor's fingers, a situation of gather—

gawkers frenetically pointing to fifty pounds of golden feather.

All the saints shrunken into postage stamps.

The bassoon laments while the dancers in nude leotards cling to the floor.

Bishops and knights retreat their queen surreptitiously, clutching their passports.

Stuck in revolving doors in a store I couldn't afford, I dislocated my warrior name while window shopping for ambition.

Someone call my supervisor in the aqua-glass skyscraper on the pretend fourteenth floor and tell him—

I'm jettisoning as we speak.

Those fabrications that filled the gaps in my resume with the fancy font have come undone.

You're a fish not a bird, he said—we can give you a promotion.

There's no equation about an echo that explains entropy.

Sunflowers wave to sloping apartment buildings and misplace melody.

None of the dolls on the slanted shelves own mouths or eyes.

How silly to linger.

Field mice are stuck in glue traps in your cellar.

How naive to pull every possible explanation down.

Who said you could shake fruit from the tree like that?

I'm here, I said—a rusted swing set, begging to pull up a chair.

For the chair to bring me a glass of water.

For the falcon to punish me for the sand I stole from the desert.

Turn me into wind that can't run hands across keys.

I didn't know how slow the death of starfish would be.

How selfish of me—thinking it was all art.

Someone will surmise, wasn't it all roundabout?

Wasn't it something? —that time travel, the holes people leave.

Someone hid the radar, wandered from glossy boardrooms where decisions are made behind closed mahogany doors.

The experts dismantled icons in Tupperware.

Components of the militia weapon were purchased online with his mother's credit card.

No one can count while that high.

There will be multiple versions of this story.

The scroll unrolled was seventy-eight feet, not eighty-seven.

The measuring stick malfunctioned.

We're singing soliloquies in a cul-de-sac, or you're having déjà vu.

Important people are sleeping.

The architect is weeping in Gothic cathedrals.

An organ has a life of its own.

Sometimes to breathe is an existential accomplishment.

Bravo!

Love is a tired camel carrying a wingless falcon to rain.

Tollbooths turning polluted water, teal.

It's better not to say so much.

It's better to ignore the wandering drones.

Your library card might be revoked.

Not all your storm windows close.

Let's play dumb like before Google became our life coach.

We could harvest our own paragraphs.

I'll sew the holes in your gray sweater in November.

We can erase the childhood trap door.

Not everyone's island will win.

Time isn't time anymore.

VI

What Was Lost

13 dancers:
August, Bunny, Canto, Fresno, Haiti, Hayden,
Hazel, Moonbeam, Orpheus, Plato, Stearns, Temple, Wolf

Unhinged from the ceiling, the gray moth was wind-scatter by Tuesday—then nothing left.

Not even a frame for a sentence-shed.

Last winter's bicycle spokes catch a hand.

Everyone in a hurry to take the remote—until then.

Orphic chords scrambled us through artery-streets in need of better armor.

Behind the TV, I'm growing pieces of music—shaken in a paper bag.

We could live on the same channels during commercials, eat the same cereal.

Now that we've grown new considerations for purple, for melody—for the play.

The theatre: misplaced and fuzzy.

One adjusts and can lurk be at the bottom of the issue—the fairy tale lesson of the castle and boat.

Don't be afraid to go alone, sorry for your tragic becoming.

Whom have you told?

Bruised humans are playing shipwreck-bumper cars to feel something, hurt someone.

One is razoring shins with trousers rolled by the carousel's sad-brown-eyed ponies.

The scent of iron can satisfy like a fact.

Lying on a bed of raven hair, Eurydice drowns images of a hand that didn't pull her to the surface.

Look at what we've done to each other while no one else was looking.

Spear fishermen risk slicing their backs on barnacle-laden rock that claims the disappearing shoreline.

It's all prehistoric—the need for slowing everything down.

Cacophony unfurls the sea's lapis lazuli, collects declarations that might or might not be expunged.

The cardinal husband and wife may have gone missing.

They only live two or three years, one of us said.

It's not your fault the winding bitterroot choked out their apple tree.

Next year the old man will chainsaw the branches and trunk in perfect increments.

It's recommended that you stay behind the dilapidated barn with the nervous horses that might get thinned out.

Until you hide the rental car, devour the elixir that could sequester you in scriptures, temporarily.

You'll regenerate completely, eventually.

Like the four-arm pink starfish Eurydice stole from the sea.

It's not a four-leaf clover, the ex-lover said.

There's no aquarium here.

The bath where I read Plato should suffice.

Where will you bathe?

The sea, of course.

Indigo nights with opaque moonlight.

The gelatinous sea animal's house detaches, but there is always a new friend.

The Book of Elucidation abandoned because there were too many pages.

Press this number to become curious again, enamored with nothing but stage—

not your obsessions, possessions, aggressions—those meticulously-ingrained habits.

Press this number when you trampoline uncontrollably out of your skin.

This number if you're feeling particularly psychotic.

The sky is untangling its grammar.

Intricate sentences will be diagrammed before erased.

We must go quickly.

Pack essentials in your torn knapsack of copious notes, your fanciful observations.

That manuscript you may never finish.

No promises.

Hurry!

It's dangerous—and stunning.

Whom have you told?

Night moves the clouds; swallows the stars we'll name for the dead while drinking cheap whisky.

None of us owns a flashlight, wood for a fire, categorical convictions.

The hours before sunrise stretch infinity, spin us sublime—

no longer overwhelmed by how limitless we've become.

Eurydice falls asleep in E Minor.

Unlike the alchemist, we wouldn't give up our families—sell food for magic.

There were many worlds within the world and outside of us, dimensions of sorrow.

To measure all of them might take eternity's windfall, truculent knowledge.

Thirteen Egyptian bulls carried the fallen troops—transformed almost everyone.

The stories became us, pages we'd sell for more bee nectar, more Himalayan blue poppies.

My mother looked in the mirror and became rain.

The house grew wings last night.

In his sleep, the beloved spoke the talk of strangers.

A boy traded his trove of baseball cards for clarity.

The pillars of some worlds would crumble.

Some days drew forever into themselves.

The papyrus folded into an origami starling that couldn't fly.

The lies professed were to maintain a semblance of normalcy while those around us schemed to sell the country.

Orpheus barters his glass lyre for an acoustic guitar; electric didn't suit him—so he can woo Eurydice back for eternity.

He strums his tapestry of poetry while silver birches drape frayed ribbons of moonlight.

Eurydice never wakes up.

Every tragic hero has the epiphany that no one can save him but himself.

Orpheus sat and wept—primal sounds under temple stones.

It's better to ignore displays of inner lives turned inside out.

No one ever knows what to say.

The spotlight tightens around Orpheus' neck when his guitar-playing arm is shorn.

Note: those who visit from the underworld can't bleed.

Some say the gods were jealous of Orpheus' heart wrenching songs.

The writers look worried.

Most of the Chorus remain calm.

Picture-window memories can be cleansed from mud and bloodshed while we wait for our subject to settle down.

Filthy blackboards thrown out definitively when the new story boards arrive.

A hero from a different tragedy carries Eurydice without waking her,

back to the afterlife before the deadline.

Redemption has its costs.

Consciousness can reset over new chasms we'll learn to navigate.

Someone should reassemble the assemblage of melodies, sequenced shards—

attach frenetic syllable-phrases to decrescendo.

Remind us what we lost, what was carelessly forgotten:

all that longing for something more.

Interlude
Spinning Ritual
Full Orchestra—Atonal

1 dancer:
Hazel

spinning buttons [string theory]   assuming [beloved]

excavating [winter's notebooks]   suspending [catastrophe]

allaying [audience discomfort]   perambulating [opaque]

gesticulating [a cab underneath]   ambuscading [megalomania]

emancipating [the frozen rabbit]   recapitulating [derailment]

butterfly-ing [ethos]   thwarting [sparrows]

charming [corroded fetishes]   voluminat-ing [protractions]

re-calculating [privacy]   provocating [dialectics]

encapsulating [abridged cartography]

circumnavigating [Saturday's crash]   feigning [Stoicism]

pirouetting [sci-fi mannequins]   spiraling [absorption]

immeasur-ating [attitude]   mitigating [solipsism]

taming [truancy] aberrant-ing [wind-decay]

engaging [betrayals]   foreplay-ing [skitter]

ferrying [mangled]   deranging [seaweed-halo]

fantasizing [consistency]   ossifying [fractals]

hang gliding [nuclear]   reconfiguring [landmines]

indelibl-ing [Runic stones]   en-cribbing [avowal]

discombobulating [tempo]   forwarding [espresso]

activating [final plans]   assuaging [magnification]

notifying [next in charge]   ameliorating [duct tape]

mitigating [kindlessness]   placating [unnamed]

explicating [disintegration]   multitasking [weeds]

fractionalizing [fractionary] re-contextualizing [wanderlust]

fraying [feather-drift]   resurrecting [road kill]

sabotaging [capacity]   extrapolating [shoe laces]

orchestrating [assemblage-machines]   replicating [nerve]

domino-ing [in Japanese]   ricocheting [birthmark]

balking [definitely]   feigning [disbelief]

threading [concrete worry beads] phishing [avatars]

imprinting [evanescence]   catfishing [diplomats]

droning [delusion]   tight-roping [faux-conduits]

jettisoning [semiotics]   triggering [excess-ion]

arbitrating [existentialism]   perpetuating [golden teeth]

fracking [atheism]   subtracting [reasonable degeneration]

mystifying [monorails] balking [debonair]

quantifying [personality]   qualifying [buttercups]

jubilat-ing [infrared]   predicating [quarks]

compulsory-izing [moonbeams]   visceral-ating [air]

rearranging [clocks]   hyperbolizing [jet stream]

placating [exiting]   re-affirming [lunch]

[intermission: 20 minutes]

If possible, don't eavesdrop on what the critics say during intermission over cappuccino and chardonnay.

Please share your impressions of the first half of this performance below and on the next page. We appreciate full sentences.

We thank you for your patronage and for your thoughtful cooperation.

[your comments continued]

Second Movement in F Major

VII

Vivifications

8 dancers:
August, Canto, Fresno, Haiti,
Hayden, Moonbeam, Stearns, Temple

Nothing actually begins the way you have it.

Just the ice cracking over old women who want to get out.

Tell them the rescue crew exploded.

Tell them anything that doesn't burn your mouth.

Someone once loved me.

Someone else pulled the trigger.

Someone climbed the stone escalators in my chest.

A new beloved arrived without umbrage.

The beloved untangled the river from sun.

Roads widened rib bones.

All my memories became radioactive.

It's excessive to take up room.

Time is an untrustworthy character, reveling in truancy.

Every language says, hello.

This is how to say, I'm frightened.

This is how to indicate distrust.

Detailed observations may prove helpful.

Some labyrinths hide dangerous spiraling.

Some thresholds cause unnecessary agitation.

Tell the mathematicians there is more than one null set.

That I was a series not a segment.

Here are my worn-out consecrations,

vestiges of divination.

They say, the anesthesia will wear off.

Your amnesia may not be a bad wrench.

We'll find you a better real estate broker.

You don't have to look so stupefied.

No one matriculated the spinout-violent scrimmage—

the let's-get-back-together tour with viable obliviousness.

Could everyone keep up?

Let's be practical.

Let's consult the playbook.

A mountain breaks the camel.

A camel becomes sounds.

Now the desert seeks new shadows.

Now the shadow takes drinks into town.

The open-mouth white lily calls cloud.

From tar roofs, mourning doves' iridescent feathers glean the sun.

The other birds become sky confetti that dreams of other birds.

In most narrations, gods are lost.

In most letters home, the war might end.

In the violet closeup spotlight—

the passed-out subject, exhausted from the interlude—

will be rescued (from parenthesis).

(Her dreaming fingers stopped weaving.)

Skins are left for new takers.

The Chorus chants holy texts in Sanskrit.

Someone should let the prisoners out.

Someone should sit down with the mother of the sociopath.

Someone should focus.

Someone should be kind.

Slowly, we fall through Celtic knots.

High-pitched animal sounds after the trap closes.

I promise to pull you from the building first.

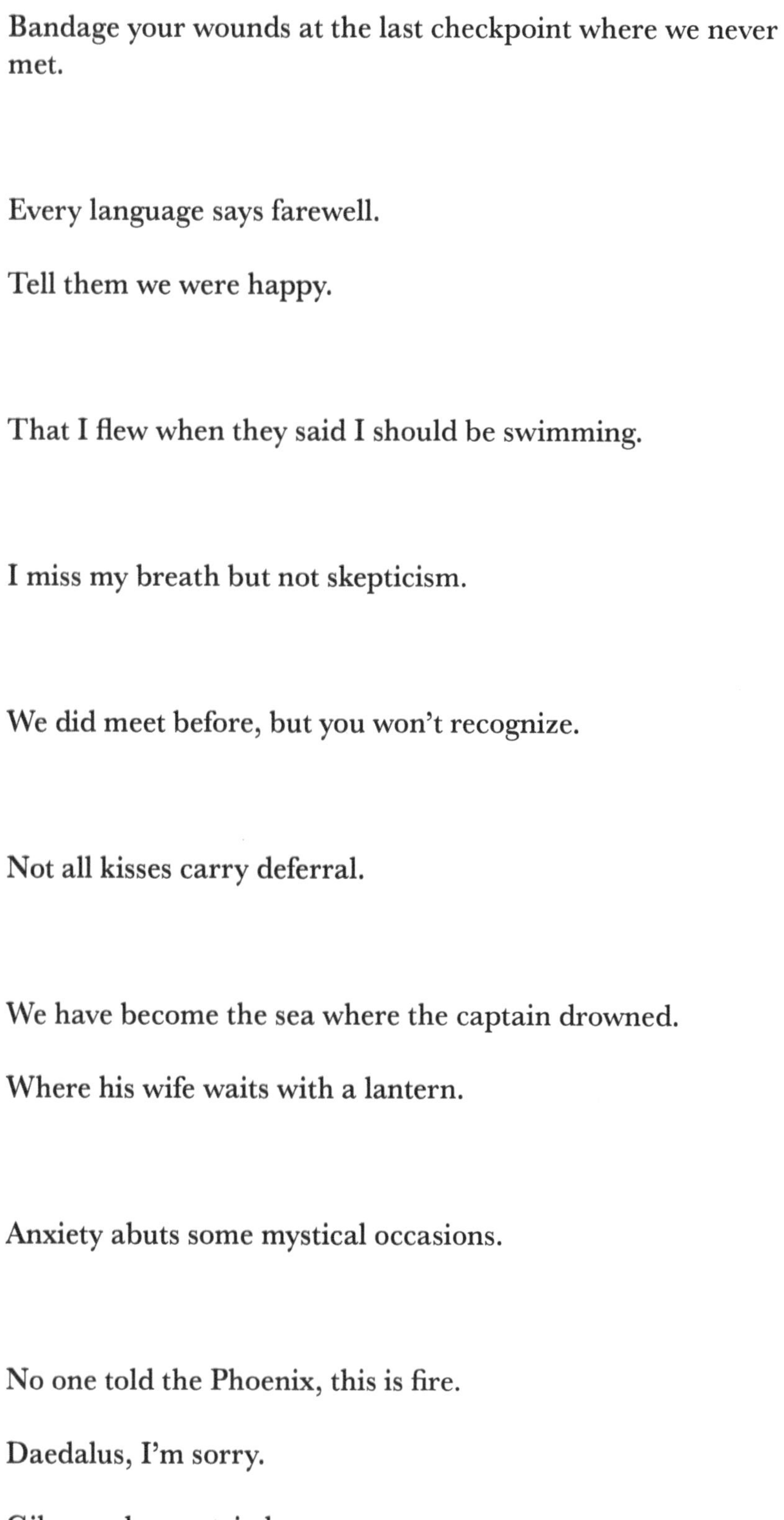

Bandage your wounds at the last checkpoint where we never met.

Every language says farewell.

Tell them we were happy.

That I flew when they said I should be swimming.

I miss my breath but not skepticism.

We did meet before, but you won't recognize.

Not all kisses carry deferral.

We have become the sea where the captain drowned.

Where his wife waits with a lantern.

Anxiety abuts some mystical occasions.

No one told the Phoenix, this is fire.

Daedalus, I'm sorry.

Gilgamesh, you tried.

Something has transmogrified.

We were shaking our own deaths with streetlight fluidity.

Everyone's pain is personal.

The Rorschach test won't help you.

Let pain be your guide, he said.

Night ended like a butterfly.

VIII

Measuring Winter

8 dancers:
Canto, Fresno, Hayden, Hazel,
Moonbeam, Plato, Stearns, Temple

We walked backwards in the blizzard thinking we missed
epiphanies.

Not comprehending until much later this was strange.

This first snow covers your footholds before I can find the house.

My skeleton key is too corroded anyway.

Thirty-three imagined steps with an unsteady gait to new
embellishments—

your brick patio of blackbirds, their blue sheen.

Are you still feeding them?

I smoked seventeen cigarettes in between sentences I'm drafting
for you.

Some stratifications piggyback infinitude like love in a
nineteenth-century novel

before someone's reputation tanks.

One goes to snow's opalescent pillows for a new rationale that specifies how.

Wing-bones rib pristine sky.

Those in warmer climates can't imagine snow.

The scrim of the inner room fading while you misdirect

an outline of feeling, not believing in belief.

Everything breaks in winter: the angel statues under pines, the washing machine, the mussel shells by the mailbox, the car.

We could live in the ice garden edged out by draping forsythia branches no one cared to cut—

in Chinese Boxes: Room of Disappearance, Room of Ephemera and Tired Verbs, Room of Bills Paid,

Room of Your Perfectionism May Be Getting in the Way—

in an Attic of Articles, House of Forgetting, Plans for Departure, an Idea of Where to Go.

The City of Z in a County of Chances in a new country where everyone reads.

Where glaciers don't melt behind church bells,

Water thrown skyward becomes ice sparrows.

Their wings snaring glints of light, glistening ice—

summon the winter sun into attention's wingspan.

Your driveway is still a sheet of ice that cracks under snowshoes.

Maybe you should put the curtains back up in your bedroom window.

Not all stalking is premeditated.

Now that ice claims the river, there is necessary mending—

the couch pillows, the holes in my stomach and brain.

The cello strings may come in handy.

Equipment set up by the side of the road calculates the impact before the crash.

A symphony beckons polyphony.

No one won the lottery tickets that fell from The Year of the Dragon piñata—

but everyone owns new socks.

The missing still gathered at the ceiling, mourning themselves.

An alternate strategy might be formulated in interstices, ellipses.

Breath that fills the sealed jar can't help anyone who loses breath,

but it's there on the mantle just in case.

With the names torn from labels, the different white pills were confused.

An abandoned bird's nest outlined in ice glistens its circular intricacy.

The miniature architect incorporating thin strips of blue and clear plastic.

When the tenor dies singing his unbeknownst swansong,

the mime will finally speak of meadows.

The dream will find the dreamer rolling dice.

We'll skate figure eights across an ethereal plane under stars subtracted by the moon emptying—

until symbols for infinity fall out of our heads.

We'll do the math later, flesh everything out, no longer self-betrayed.

Time cast against the other three dimensions—

the poetic field: a helix and ellipse.

The videographer transformed our own euphoria.

You said the night was beautiful.

That there were diamonds in my hair.

The panda cub in China somersaults new snow hills and doesn't appear to be lonely in this instance.

Siamese twins fantasize privacy.

It's become possible to live within complexities that no one will fathom.

The audience wants transparency not murkiness,

but intention can be unkind.

The yardstick couldn't measure the nor'easter with all that wind.

Against the cold, our skeletons fold in.

A handful of officials were subpoenaed for a breach of intelligence,

exiled without surveillance.

The promised test results disclose an uncomfortable atrophy—knowledge of the rotting shed.

When your situation flourishes more robustly,

we'll send notification to affected parties, C.O.D., concerning your spiritual dishevelment.

Expect an important announcement or memo—something unequivocal.

Ha-ha.

There'll be more agenda items to cover, examine, sign off on.

Ink is preferable in most scenarios, but for how long no one can say per the way of carbon paper and cursive.

It's essential to dig out from layers of languishing.

A relinquishing of representation might identify a miraculous golden thread

to sew wounds it might be preferable to staple or ignore--

all those tenacious criticisms, snubs.

I was trying to pour toxicity and ego into a bottle of perfume.

I was trying to become myself.

I saved the transcription of your under-the-covers voice in my fireproof hope chest.

It won't be long until the hour undoes itself, the appointment evaporates from the waiting room.

Thirteen yellowed teeth will go missing from the frozen piano.

The orchestra, interpretive and unsettled, expands theater constructed for philosophers.

Conceptual art at its finest.

When you're not around, they'll tell you the tree fell in the forest.

To stay calm, one could focus on theoretical symmetry.

Afternoon stuck itself in the cogwheels of morning.

Impatient inhabitants hasten toward something more reasonable.

Unable to bear tragedy, the composer is hungry for a new score,

but his ducks aren't in a row—

Duck A, duck D, Z, 8, duck of A Minor, G Minor, B flat, golden duck, rubber duck, emerald duck,

duck that can't be killed by the hunter treading the landscape's edges.

His poker face perfected when the clouds take on sun.

The vertigo will lessen in the coming days when the wavelength of the weekend finds its divot.

When sleep still won't take you, count three thousand birds in the ancient Persian text—

flying without you.

Six thousand wings evaporating when you wake.

We should walk together out of this melting land, holding hands until the southern border.

The forecasters predict sleet, but it feels like snow.

We mustn't speak of any of this.

IX

Erasures of Triangles

3 dancers:
Hazel, Plato, Wolf

The violins, piccolos, and violas converse intensely before the oboe interrupts—

flat lines the tempo, mood shift.

The way a plane abandons sound.

The brass on hold—extraterrestrial high-pitched chanting.

Some sounds affect the crowd.

Some want to awkwardly crawl home.

The evaporating field of distance opens gaps in thinking.

You know.

The "y" on the graph didn't want a wrought-iron frame for fate's uncertain footage.

In the next century they'll use micro-tweezers

to pluck painful flashbacks and thoughts out of the brain.

Maybe they won't know PTSD, anxiety, or that--

Plato misspoke.

Wittgenstein couldn't find his trousers because there were too many shelves.

Derrida buttered his toast.

Pythagoras had an aversion to beans.

Euclid went mad.

Wolf vanished inside a sentence.

Jilted Sappho gifted the ocean with fragment-stone.

Prufrock ate a nectarine.

Stein's little dog didn't know her but liked roses.

Penelope finished the burial shroud for Laertes, allowing the most handsome suitor to unpin her silver hair.

Odysseus clung to Argos, believing he was a goddess.

Atlas said, ENOUGH.

The sun lost her fingers.

Mars no longer longed to be crimson or misunderstand Venus.

Pluto's father told him, life isn't fair.

Everyone was playing nice with their hands buried in dirt.

Pretending not to be bored.

Pretending the orchestra caged suffering.

Canto jounces apple branches for fun.

Albee admits he's the one afraid.

Beckett ups the ante.

We're watching you bandage your Achilles' heel for tonight's unraveling.

Ophelia's long, copper hair flowing under forget-me-nots in a photograph.

Those aren't the right clothes for a curbside funeral, but red suits you.

No one knew the captain absconded from his hallucinations.

That the ghost ship knew him better than anyone—that he preferred planes.

He couldn't come clean, start over.

Some souvenirs aren't recyclable because chaos reifies us on repeat.

Intentions can't move triangles because triangles can't move beliefs,

curl methodology.

While I unplugged, went green, ignored everyone—

comedy masks, elegant and glittery, and grotesque tragedy masks—

fell from dinner parties into sewer drains.

The Grand Puppeteer severed all strings.

Master, how could you do this to me?

So you would dream.

Forgotten Countries

10 dancers:
August, Canto, Fresno, Haiti, Hayden,
Hazel, Moonbeam, Orpheus, Stearns, Temple

None of the survivors could speak when the press arrived.

The makeup on the reporters' faces—jarring.

It was still a rescue search.

Pinged on their phones, the journalists jetted to another country.

Most media viewers can handle only one catastrophe at a time.

Even though the world constricted, a dull bell jar with various tunnels of ants.

The new headline: a throwback to another stampede.

Take me.

Some will be tortured, but this report won't travel.

When the children questioned the vanishing of high-tech camera equipment,

no one could explain the stigma of poverty.

A dollar is still a dollar, someone said.

The aftermath smells like bleach that burns closed eyes.

A red line evaporates.

The boy with one leg studies the war zone from his bombed-out apartment's fifth floor,

hoping to see his soccer ball.

Wizening men may someday disclose the war to themselves in open spaces, eat rice again.

Not everyone wants to hear about napalm.

The living will was necessary by all accounts.

A small girl paints orange rain not knowing it's fire.

Her father tells her that goldfish are jumping from the sky.

After the genocide, I buried the Book of the Dead because there were too many.

The writing in a different language on white body bags will be confused.

No one knows the proper names.

Someone might write: she was brave, his hands were tied behind his back, this wasn't supposed to happen.

this is a baby, a mother, an old woman, a teenage soldier, a journalist who stayed behind.

We held charms to ward off evil spirits—

a talisman, amulet, fetish, unblinking evil eye, flattened marble,

golden toads, worry dolls, three-legged pigs.

Don't take me forever.

No one knows me yet.

The wind hid behind those gathered around the burning effigy of the dictator—

greedy for even a partial catharsis.

All of this made us very tired.

While everyone was throwing sugared candy at the parade of saints,

life-size puppets go rogue—

jump a train, bohemians seeking seafarer trajectories.

They fumble for an eternity until they find work and a family.

A half-dozen or so buckle under the new kind of choosing and even with lifelines—

can't be saved, get out of bed.

Low cards shuffled neurotically examined genetic codes.

What's a six to an Ace, a seven to a King?

Let's go nuclear, he said—but the general knocked him down.

The eye-level, pale full moon ascended before dusk,

edging out the burning sun.

We’re writing a new history of dolls that when tilted,

their eyes don’t close.

Night’s velvet wings, folding down, nest the horizon.

Tomorrow I’ll write notations that no one can summarize.

XI

Book of Missing Wings

9 dancers:
August, Bunny, Fresno, Haiti,
Hayden, Hazel, Plato, Stearns, Wolf

How odd that we walk under the same sky but are so different.

Some of us desired aloneness—that feeling of omission from the pack.

Being can be so selfish.

I've misfiled passion or it fled, said it couldn't look at me this way.

I was afraid to open this Book.

Afraid the pages would be empty—

of being estranged, the ending, Icarus' demise.

The Achilles' heel returned in a shoebox coffin lined with scarlet silk.

The succulence of honeysuckle and jasmine rescinded.

A subtraction of the infinite at the neighborhood barbecue.

The wrong small talk for every occasion, maybe
phenomenology, the wrong clothes.

The lake dreamed of waves and the ocean, stillness.

The woman became stuck in a statue.

High tide took her, all arms.

She was no Galatea.

Alabaster drowns.

Love is not a Subaru even driving up snow mountains.

Fractures will require resetting after collapsing windpipes.

Deep in dream, the dog biting its owner—a concern.

Don't ask too many questions.

In a black and white film, the hero swims through clouds.

She was tired.

She pushed on the gas.

She opened air.

Someone else's tragedy can be so interesting.

One lands at one point—and another, another.

I was counting green lights, watery in the rain's reflection,

hugging narrowing turns.

Maybe the pedal stuck, maybe an object I can't remember.

No headlights, for some reason, guardrails missing.

The pills in the car because I couldn't sleep all summer.

Underwater blood, thin jellyfish, then pink swirls,

dissolving into inkwell.

No pages in the car salvageable—

even when hung out on a stranger's clothesline.

White rectangular flags of surrender, blurring gray.

They say 260 miles per hour, but I don't believe them.

I unfurled the long parchment, terrified that I would be effaced.

Wouldn't understand anything after effulgence abraded.

Nervous there were no steady signs to follow—

that I'll forget something useful: how to button a shirt,

fold down its collar, learn how to use the new phone.

Time rains clarinets in a manuscript.

When the dust settles there will be more dust.

We can adapt to mostly anything—even a quiet disappointment

that events didn't go our way.

Here's a consolation prize: free tickets to an amusement park or an Italian film, depending on your mood—

a feather pen from the seabird that misjudged the cliffs, the peacock at the petting zoo that disappeared.

The frozen, dead rabbit was not an omen, but we didn't tell anyone.

Bunny, we hope it happened fast.

We covered her with velour blankets underneath two feet of snow—until the thicket thawed for a proper burial underneath white lilies.

Wolf, remorseful at the stream.

Vectors dance circular, though not all subjects of the study

could be resurrected gracefully.

A brochure indicated that the artist's new sculpture was eleven stories high.

Only helicopters could properly view it—circle metal and glass.

An architect constructed a demo with extra-large fuchsia lingerie.

In a crowded parking lot, an abstract expressionist pushes his unfinished painting uphill.

We want to tell him the canvas, expanding, is beautiful, but early night begins its spilling—

and we can't decide how to fill anything in.

We woke without remembering all disclosure is personal.

Tried to disregard anti-chronologically.

It wasn't your fault.

Tripping over your desk with absurdity.

Thursday swept you under the Persian rug.

You should admit at the meeting that you're ill-prepared

while securing a lane for everyone's bullshit.

The emerald slipper, by pure miracle, resurfaced by the dogwood tree.

Research indicates that with hours of consistent practice, ghosts can move objects—

but can't touch human bodies or hair.

Socks and postage stamps would continue to go missing.

It's okay, the ghost of the house said in honey-whisper.

Your father's voice still on the answering machine.

The girl, naming carrier pigeons, should come down from the peaked tar roof of the Victorian house of childhood:

Toby, Bob, Amelia, August, Sandwich.

Don't touch them, her mother said—they carry disease.

But their claws delivered fortunes to those lost under bridges.

The planes flew through your chest at high speed because someone called you Sky—

and you believed.

No one onboard except robots practicing miniature military schemes,

searching satellites.

You're boasting you're telepathic, and we're deeply concerned.

No one had the heart to tell you that light didn't need us.

That the field of yellow buttercups indicated we were all lying.

Valerian root might calm you down, but you might hover above your body—

half-dreaming.

You'll remember the ancient tablets, lost magical birds.

Even though the stones have crumbled into sharp small slabs—

the words, when rearranged, stay the same.

Ideas of a shining place weren't formulated in a day.

I was memorizing something to tell you, but it fell apart.

There were intricate ways to express one thing, but no way to account for everything.

I might sew you a quilt if the sewing machine doesn't stitch my fingers,

compose a symphony that offers movement—

backlit with your own refulgence,

Tempered by your fear of wandering too far.

The lecture on neuroplasticity didn't explain anything about spirituality.

Deities should then be removed from the Book in the form of a question.

Scientists claim that without a cerebral cortex, fish can't cry—

but poets know their tears fill rivers.

The House becomes a main character because it needs so much —

absorbing us into sheetrock not windows.

Someone will make the bed thinking about minutiae, then morphology,

the pathology of someone else's disease—

the ceiling where the ghosts eventually leave.

Some of us were living in square houses even though we were circles.

The traveling philosopher reassured things would get better before he fell off the grid.

He didn't charge us; didn't covet any of our possessions.

His mother, a soprano, died singing an aria to a sold-out audience.

She was a circle, he said.

The director wept for a year, a small fishpond that grew lily pads and moss.

I haven't listened to your messages because I can't remember which Rooms are private.

Most of us agree I'm not sleepwalking underwater—

but swimming without sound through watercolors.

Through blue, I'll swim through yellow to green, maybe red—

pretend enthusiasm.

When you come back, we'll tango in slow-motion—

knowing love isn't a small boat on a lake of promises.

Heartbreak ensconces endlessly.

You missed your appointment with the person who was supposed to help you,

an aloof hawk in search of a new paradigm.

At night you hold me against the river-rush and wash my oily hair.

You'll feel better, you said.

The Chorus circumscribes us.

Others are choosing a novel typescript—

a single path out of the courtroom.

They're winning something over in a final hour.

Studying what was sacrificed.

The manager at the menial job told him he was so smart, he was stupid.

Things didn't go well after that.

While cows found tree hollow, I tented the hillside in the rain
with the loneliness of actuaries, widows, and scholars.

The bear cub should be drinking the brook without car traffic.

The one-year-old brown moose shouldn't be swimming in the canal.

No one prepared properly for so much erosion.

No one noticed you talked faster.

No one wanted to know how many bullet holes.

No one prepared for complications and played dead once more

—too tired for commentary or composure.

Hadn't it been so grandiose?

Vanity pulled out all the stops.

Your ego, a flattened tire discarded in the woods—

permits an invention of a sacred shrine, or maybe just a new floor.

The ship left the party on the pontoon boat.

It took a new Book to return us to ourselves.

I'm one of you, I swear.

There's dirt under our fingernails and in our mouths—

dissolution, disillusion distillation, dissuasion, deluge, debacle, decay.

We're longing for a simplified list of truths while gardeners dream of winter.

Their fireplace chimneys cleaned of baby bats sleeping in squirrel nests.

Symmetrical swallowtails found the fennel with infrared.

Blackbirds with serrated wings found your house.

Neither symbolic, but otherworldly.

The lightning bugs and emerald-bellied hummingbirds left us with tree frogs.

The thing I wanted to tell you, it turns out, isn't one thing, and will upset you, I said.

Then let's tell lies, he said, or talk like strangers.

The House grew wings again last night, he said.

I don't have an unholy sense of aloneness, I said.

I know where I'm going.

Some afternoons flow.

My pain threshold is growing.

I didn't draw the Death card.

When pillars of the foundation were removed succinctly,

stone sentinels in repose—the audience wept holes.

You should know.

Maybe I lit the fire.

Maybe I dreamed I was awake.

We were renaming alibis, trading documents too dangerous to read.

A new game to entertain fugitives.

No one said, it's your turn to tightrope across.

That time is a mess, spiraling.

That a picture won't comply.

Sixteenth notes took melancholy.

No one knew exactly.

No one said the story might notice itself.

Tomorrow I'll memorize your expressions, cracks when you cower,

or laugh—

never mentioning the conversations we buried.

There's no container for memory.

I was no longer in disagreement with myself—

holding an omnipotent grudge.

We were tallying loose ends to send a clearer postcard.

Not much has happened all at once.

XII

Amplifications

9 dancers:
August, Canto, Fresno, Haiti,
Hayden, Hazel, Plato, Stearns, Temple

The composition ruptures, spills—causes teetering.

Not everyone will cooperate with effectiveness.

Talk wanted to talk about itself.

The subject of the story will say, no—

held hostage in a reverberating explanation.

There was no translation when it was sung.

The vaulted ceilings amplified a DIRGE for mortality, a lament for not coming back.

The Chorus stayed very quiet, balanced on pins—

contemplating vertically.

Freesia became wind.

Confidentiality obliterated.

Our watches are broken, and mourning doves need more time
on gray roofs.

The garden was betrayed for sorrow.

It can own you sometimes.

Despair has a resume a mile long.

Unlike the dog, the brain couldn't be taught to sit.

Morning glories, striped violet and white, climbing the privacy
wall—

have closed without sun.

Moonflowers preen white trumpet blooms, hallucinogenic.

Night smells like heliotrope.

Small perpendicular houses were almost sleeping.

Dormers tightened over green-stained aluminum ledges,

Years of rain nestled in.

Voyeurism isn't always creepy, she said—I wanted to see how someone else lived.

The middle-aged man counts his money in the freezer.

Ballet dancers don't have one leg shorter.

Spines lack symmetry, vertebrae leaning—

one's backbone in ugly situations can cave.

That was before the ethical fallout, before the police arrived.

Maybe the prescribed pills were too many.

Scientists are trying to determine if humans need cranial magnets or touch.

Someone loved before less mattered.

Facts often act factually.

Notes needed endnotes to understand this many layers of longing.

But that might be a tomorrow thing.

All our fingerprints are different, every voice, each eye—how
unfathomable, the boy said to impress the girl

while they surfed subway turnstiles.

That was when he had two legs, but no one explains.

Some of us liked each other.

Some of us pretended because it was easier.

Some of us wept behind picnic benches.

Small children know mostly none of this.

No one talks about how we've misplaced the TV.

No one should panic.

We lost the oars.

Immortality might be a passageway of calcium.

This time wear black.

This time don't say you're sorry.

By the time you read this,

a strange music fills the unfamiliar room.

It's not all that much but strangely enough.

Some days end before they begin.

We're voting if this act is over.

The chorus is weighing in.

XIII

Tangerine Symphony

13 dancers:
August, Bunny, Canto, Fresno, Haiti, Hayden,
Hazel, Moonbeam, Orpheus, Plato, Stearns, Temple, Wolf

Friday shuffled the rain's pages.

Saturday threw a lifeline to resurrect dreaming.

The sun's image fits in a miniature dollhouse's tiny white frame.
The rainmaker leaves Nevada for Seattle, dyes her hair pink—

and focuses on climate change.

You should dead-bolt your front door—

the circus is in town.

The celebration will still occur in the morning,

guests wearing run-on sentences.

It's a new thing.

There was a memo about the string section, wind instruments,
and oddly, trees.

I should apologize that my long-winded rebuttal burst into
flames

after my first I'm sorry email infected your hard drive.

No one was supposed to bleed on shrill speed.

I lost the lines you were waiting for—

spent your money on champagne.

It's the rain's fault, its breath on orange rose petals.

The fog at night that swallows highways.

I sent away for the starter happiness kit,

but my debit card was declined.

I lacked mooring until someone explained counterpoint.

Now that focus is realigned, there's a renewed enchantment for
nasturtium and marigolds.

Buckets left for hoarding blazoned sun.

Disillusionment hinges with clocks,

but you're overqualified to decorate doubt.

There's a free hotline for an existential quandary.

Worn-out theories can be returned express mail, postage paid.

Now that your avatar is role-playing.

Shortfalls of logic become pillows when voices clamor against the slate of darkness.

Sleep doesn't always give back dream in slow-motion montage.

Not everything can be reassembled.

Modern dancers transform the stage without cue.

The priest arrives with a suitcase of benedictions before the dancers' I / we / you crash.

Unwittingly, the Chorus deconstructs.

It's time to find the way back somewhere we might remember.

Consult the travel log, map of second or tenth chances,

alternate scenario-riffs.

There were more feathers to nail into mechanical wings that would flap,

lopsided angels looming above the children's scarecrows.

The ghosts say, go slow.

Tomorrow you won't obsess about obsessing.

Someone in the suburbs shrugs that none of this matters,

but we can edit that out later.

Some of us are nervous—hinging small deaths without stalemate.

Experiences can occur with or without us.

When this is over, I'll make new friends, eat tangerines and kale,

purchase a durable watch with indiglo, all-weather hiking boots.

I'll read Infinite Jest and Crime and Punishment,

return all the overdue C.S. Lewis books on grieving and theology, learn Sanskrit.

I'll restring my cello.

I might stop lying.

But I'm too preoccupied with growing falcon wings to conduct a new kind of symphony.

Night after night, strange sequences—

when my dreams dream without me.

I'll believe in a happy ending.

The dying woman's dreams will fill her wardrobe.

I'll pen you notes from where we've been.

CODA
a cappella

2 dancers:
Hazel, Moonbeam

I don't recall how the fire ended—how blue flames maneuvered the midpoint.

How parchment pages ignited, left white ash in our hair on Saturday.

The ghost of my father untangled my hair with a golden brush.

Shhh, he wept—but it's all so convoluted.

Moonlight bathed me in sheaths of gossamer for an endless stretch of hours—or one expansive night that approximates infinity.

I can't tell.

Before the trumpets and final cymbal crash—

I wake up—alive.

But on the next page, everyone is gone.

Afterword

Krysia Jopek

I slept without dreaming the summer of 2021.

Morning after morning, before having coffee, before both feet were back in the waking world—I told myself that I slept in the Book of the Dead.

This assertion was strange as I had never read the Book of the Dead or taught any selections from it that I can remember.

I started listening to the Egyptian Book of the Dead at night, but still—no dreaming. Research led me to the second translation of the title: Book Emerging Forth into Light.

The Egyptian Book of the Dead/Book Emerging Forth into Light was read by a high priest to the dying to accompany/escort them from the earthly realm to the afterlife.

Though I didn't dream all summer, I started writing DIRGE: a ballet for 13 dancers in the mornings while sitting on a doorstep that faced my patio garden with a backdrop of early-morning birdsong.

I knew that I wanted to write one poetic composition, one book in 13 parts, that could also be performed. I had no idea that writing this book would take me on such a journey (often thrilling and often involving long hours of painstakingly hard work) that would take almost two years to complete.

I don't remember why I chose the title DIRGE. Was I writing a lament for missing dreams, a lament for being human and all that entails,

an elegy for those who have left the earthly realm for an unknown afterlife, those who have died mourning the physical, sensory world,

a hymn or series of hymns that allow the reader to experience an artistic event through language that offers some catharsis and perhaps spirituality, a partial reprieve from everyday temporal existence?

I think these are questions for the reader to answer.

Windsor, Connecticut, February 2024

Meditation On DIRGE

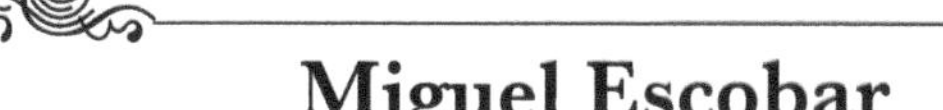

Miguel Escobar

Do we enter looking back imagining in one instant over a thousand permutations on the tongue, burnt bridges into a first afterlife? Cohesion, coherence, correlation, any one or all may become suspect, put up on the shelf, quaint, outmoded institutions.

Does what masquerades as thickly veiled ballet become stealthy vehicle for building a bonfire underneath microcosm? Time bending while time refusing to accept time may have after all stood still.

An elusive cognition both teasing and tempting, where absence of longing shows itself to be the embodiment of everything longed for, everything soon to be missed, the apparent absence of tears, despair, melancholy a curious, almost palatable harbinger of final, grudging, or even relief-laden acceptance.

Language an innate power veering off on pathways away from nostalgic clinging to the immediate or necessary conclusion, away from the normal present of behaving tenses, the entirely parasitic future, the unknown afterlife—taking us where, exactly?

Its own sublime, diverse beauty, something organic in a free wielding of experimental mindset—a choreographed space to enter.

Miguel Escobar
Sacramento, California, USA

DIRGE: A ballet for 13 dancers as Performance

Mike Cole

It is Krysia Jopek's intention that DIRGE: a ballet for 13 dancers be performed as a contemporary "hybrid" ballet complete with 13 dancers, background music, and a Chorus (think of a Greek Chorus) reading (or singing) their lines as the dancers emerge into the light and recede back into the darkness as we might imagine figures would during a voyage down the mythical river Styx that flowed (perhaps still flows) between the land of the living and the realm of the dead.

While Jopek's book, one long composition comprised of a prelude, thirteen acts, and a coda, does not relate a narrative in the traditional sense, the organizational thread is that of dreams in which images, words, and phrases that might seem random nevertheless have a powerful continuity that, as dreams can, might startle us frightfully awake or leave us after our night of sleep with a fearful uneasiness that might last well into a day or beyond.

DIRGE is meant to be performed and recited aloud so that the images and insights can resonate as the voices and visions in dreams do, putting our lives, our presence here in the land of the living, in the context of all who have gone before us and who travel with us through the shattered and scattered realities of our being.

Not all in DIRGE is fearful and ominous. The speakers in Jopek's full-length book of poetry are survivors who know that the only way to confront and rise above the horrors and seemingly inevitable self-destruction of our kind is to find pleasure and even humor in the play of language and in putting historical or mythic characters in new contexts that help us see that we needn't take ourselves or our supposed heroes and superiors so seriously that we lose the capacity to enjoy and celebrate the light that is always there for us as a counterpoint to the darkness on that "other side of the river."

Throughout our history, we have been telling each other variations of the same stories that are meant to inspire us and encourage us toward the greater good, but those narratives have not prevented humans from repeating the offenses against each other and against the natural world that have brought us ever closer to our own extinction. Maybe it is time to find a different way of seeing our shared experience and of recognizing the fallacies and even dangers in following formulaic ways of trying to understand and come to terms with who and what we are.

In all the arts, the move toward nonlinear, non-narrative language, imagery, and performance has offered alternative ways of understanding who we are and how we can best see and be in our world—how we can best escape despair. Think of the poems of Gertrude Stein, John Cage's non-music, Jackson Pollock's abstract paintings, the work of contemporary sculptors. et al. DIRGE represents one of Krysia Jopek's attempts to carry that new way of seeing forward.

Short of attending a "hybrid" formal performance of DIRGE: a ballet of 13 dancers, I would encourage you, if you want to experience Jopek's book fully, to bring a group of friends together to read the book aloud because it is intended to be spoken and felt as the verses of the wandering poets of antiquity were. Or, you can listen to poet Miguel Escobar's beautiful and haunting recording of DIRGE at 2ndEcho.bandcamp.com

Listening to Escobar's recording of DIRGE is a perfect way to develop a deeper understanding of what Jopek has achieved in DIRGE and seeing how her work links with both ancient and more modern poetic traditions, especially the oral traditions that have existed throughout time and are evidenced in our modern world in everything from religious chants and recitations of many cultures to present day spoken word and performance poetry. The sound and rhythm of her work need to be heard and felt for the poetry to come fully alive and to be fully experienced.

Enjoy your voyage through DIRGE. Hopefully, you will emerge from the experience in the mood to celebrate the wonders of this shared passage through our frightening and often distressing but still miraculously lovely and endlessly illuminating and surprising world.

Mike Cole
Ahwahnee, California

Acknowledgments

Sincere eternal gratitude to Kurt Lovelace, publisher and founder of **Pierian Springs Press**, for designing **DIRGE: A BALLET FOR 13 DANCERS** in such a beautiful format. I can't thank him enough for his patience, as **DIRGE** evolved over a longer time period than anticipated.

DIRGE wouldn't be the book it is without the feedback, cheerleading, suggestions for editing, and proofreading from poet/editor Mike Cole and poet/voice performer Miguel Escobar. Their enthusiasm for this project and my poetics was infectious. I listened to Miguel's October 2022 professional recording of **DIRGE** many times, which influenced revisions over the next two months. Mike and Miguel taught me about what resonated with them, potential readers, as **DIRGE** burgeoned into its final iteration. I can't thank them enough for their profuse time and energy.

In section V., ***Feathers of Yellow Wings Desire Thumbprints***—I have to credit Thom Foster for the amazing line, "Icarus never wept," a title he gave me for a poem upon my request that I wove into **DIRGE** instead.

In section XI., ***Book of Missing Wings***—Kristen Anderson is the architect who constructed an installation from extra-large fuchsia lingerie for an architecture project at Rensselaer Polytechnic Institute.

Reading from **DIRGE** (in progress) in January 2022 for SpoFest, curated by James Bryant, offered a platform and motivation to solidify the opening sections, which built important momentum for the manuscript. SpeakEasy Café, hosted by Nyla Alisia. also provided a live audience for sections of **DIRGE**, honed to read on several of her weekly poetry talk radio shows.

Lastly, I'm grateful to those not mentioned yet who continue to inspire me: Sheikha A, Sam Beckett, J Karl Bogartte, Gordon Hilgers, Dale Houstman, Khader Humied, Sharon Lattig, Peter Di Pietro, Chris Stroffolino, Michael Todd, and Paulette Turcotte.

Krysia Jopek

Windsor, Connecticut, May 2024

Krysia Jopek

Krysia Jopek earned her Bachelor's Degree and Master's Degree in English from the **University of Connecticut**, her Master's of Philosophy in Poetics and Twentieth-Century American Poetry from the **City University of New York Graduate Center**, and a Master's of Fine Arts in Literary Fiction from **Albertus Magnus.**

She studied in London her sophomore year at the **University of Connecticut** and attended *Semester at Sea* through the **University of Pittsburgh** during the fall semester of her senior year before teaching writing and world literature at **City College of New York** for a decade. The combination of her family background, travels, education, and teaching brings a global dimension to her writing and worldview.

Her father's family survived deportation from Poland to Siberia by Stalin in 1940 and remained Displaced Persons until 1952, which is the subject of her novel, MAPS AND SHADOWS (Aquila Polonica, 2010), recipient of a ***Silver Benjamin Franklin Award*** in Historical Fiction. She is also the maternal granddaughter of Polish immigrants.

Her chapbook, HOURGLASS STUDIES (Crisis Chronicles, 2017), a single poem in 12 sections, was nominated for a Pushcart Award in Poetry. She has written reviews of contemporary poetry for *The American Book Review*, *The Pacific Rim of Books*, and *Canadian Poetry Review*. Her poems have appeared in *BlazeVox*, *Redactions*, *The Wallace Stevens Journal*, and *Columbia Poetry Review*, among other journals. In 2017 she founded ***Diaphanous Micro***, an e-journal of literary and visual art. She currently resides in Connecticut.

Also by Krysia Jopek

Fiction

MAPS AND SHADOWS
Aquila Polonica, 2010

Winner of the
Silver Benjamin Franklin Award
in Historical Fiction

Poetry Chapbooks

HOURGLASS STUDIES
Crisis Chronicles, 2017

www.ingramcontent.com/pod-product-compliance
Lightning Source LLC
Chambersburg PA
CBHW030553310726
48979CB00011B/2133/J

* 9 7 8 1 9 5 3 1 3 6 0 5 3 *